A Note from
Mary Pope Osborne About the

MAGIC TREE HOUSE® FACT TRACKERS

When I write Magic Tree House® adventures, I love including facts about the times and places Jack and Annie visit. But when readers finish these adventures, I want them to learn even more. So that's why we write a series of nonfiction books that are companions to the fiction titles in the Magic Tree House® series. We call these books Fact Trackers because we love to track the facts! Whether we're researching dinosaurs, pyramids, Pilgrims, sea monsters, or cobras, we're always amazed at how wondrous and surprising the real world is. We want you to experience the same wonder we do—so get out your pencils and notebooks and hit the trail with us. You can be a Magic Tree House® Fact Tracker, too!

Mary Pope Osborne

Here's what kids, parents, and teachers have to say about the Magic Tree House® Fact Trackers:

"They are so good. I can't wait for the next one. All I can say for now is prepare to be amazed!" —Alexander N.

"I have read every Magic Tree House book there is. The [Fact Trackers] are a thrilling way to get more information about the special events in the story." —John R.

"These are fascinating nonfiction books that enhance the magical time-traveling adventures of Jack and Annie. I love these books, especially *American Revolution*. I was learning so much, and I didn't even know it!" —Tori Beth S.

"[They] are an excellent 'behind-the-scenes' look at what the [Magic Tree House fiction] has started in your imagination! You can't buy one without the other; they are such a comple- ment to one another." —Erika N., mom

"Magic Tree House [Fact Trackers] took my children on a journey from Frog Creek, Pennsylvania, to so many significant historical events! The detailed manuals are a remarkable addition to the classic fiction Magic Tree House books we adore!" —Jenny S., mom

"[They] are very useful tools in my classroom, as they allow for students to be part of the planning process. Together, we find facts in the [Fact Trackers] to extend the learning introduced in the fictional companions. Researching and planning classroom activities, such as our class Olympics based on facts found in *Ancient Greece and the Olympics*, help create a genuine love for learning!" —Paula H., teacher

FACT TRACKER

Titanic

A NONFICTION COMPANION TO MAGIC TREE HOUSE #17:

Tonight on the *Titanic*

BY WILL OSBORNE
AND MARY POPE OSBORNE

ILLUSTRATED BY SAL MURDOCCA

A STEPPING STONE BOOK™

Random House 🏠 New York

The Magic Tree House Fact Tracker series was formerly known
as the Magic Tree House Research Guide series.

Visit us on the Web!
SteppingStonesBooks.com
MagicTreeHouse.com

Educators and librarians, for a variety of teaching tools, visit us at
RHTeachersLibrarians.com

Library of Congress Cataloging-in-Publication Data
Osborne, Will.
Titanic / by Will Osborne and Mary Pope Osborne ;
illustrated by Sal Murdocca.
   p. cm. — (Magic tree house fact tracker)
ISBN 978-0-375-81357-3 (trade) — ISBN 978-0-375-91357-0 (lib. bdg.) —
ISBN 978-0-307-97519-5 (ebook)
1. *Titanic* (Steamship)—Juvenile literature. 2. Shipwrecks—North Atlantic Ocean—
Juvenile literature. 3. Survival after airplane accidents, shipwrecks, etc.—Juvenile literature.
I. Osborne, Mary Pope. II. Murdocca, Sal, ill.
III. Title.
GR530.T6 O63 2011 910.9163'4—dc22 2010052316

Printed in the United States of America
43 42 41 40 39 38 37 36 35 34

This book has been officially leveled by using the F&P Text Level Gradient™
Leveling System.

For Joe Harmston

Historical Consultant:
KAREN KAMUDA, Vice President, The Titanic Historical Society Inc.*, and Publisher, *The Titanic Commutator*

Education Consultant:
MELINDA MURPHY, Media Specialist, Reed Elementary School, Cypress Fairbanks Independent School District, Houston, Texas

Once again, special thanks to Paul Coughlin for his ongoing photographic contribution to the series and to our superb creative team at Random House: Joanne Yates, Helena Winston, Diane Landolf, Cathy Goldsmith, Mallory Loehr, and as always, our wonderful editor, Shana Corey.

TITANIC

Contents

Dear Readers,

We came back from our journey in _Tonight on the Titanic_ with lots of questions. How was the _Titanic_ different from other ships? Who was traveling on the ship? Why did the _Titanic_ sink? Why weren't more people rescued?

To find out the answers to these questions, we had to be fact trackers!

We went to the library. We found books with photographs of the _Titanic_ and its passengers. We checked out a DVD that told us how the _Titanic_ sank. We found a website with a _Titanic_ timeline, and another with stories told by people who survived the disaster.

Now we want to share the facts with you.

So get your notebook, get your backpack, and get ready to set sail on your own voyage of <u>Titanic</u> fact-tracking.

Jack

Annie

1

The Biggest Ship in the World

In the early 1900s there were no airplanes. The only way to get across the ocean was by ship.

In 1906, a British company called the Cunard (kyoo-NARD) Line launched two new ships. The ships were large and comfortable. They could cross the Atlantic Ocean in five days. They quickly became the most popular ocean liners in the world.

Large passenger ships that travel on the open seas are called <u>ocean liners</u>.

A few years later, news of three new ocean liners began to spread around the world. These ships were being built for a company called the White Star Line. The White Star ships would not be quite as fast as the Cunard ships, but they would be much larger and fancier. Some people called them "floating palaces."

Titanic means "huge and powerful."

One of these floating palaces was the *Titanic*.

14

It took more than two years to build the *Titanic*. When the ship was finished, it was as long as three football fields. It was as tall as an 11-story building. It had room on board for more than 2,500 passengers. It was the biggest ship in the world.

In Greek mythology, the <u>Titans</u> were a race of giants.

Titanic

Long as three football fields

Tall as 11-story building

Room for 2,500+ passengers

Thomas Andrews

Much of the planning of the *Titanic* was done by a man named Thomas Andrews. Andrews tried to

The <u>Titanic</u> was built at a shipyard in Belfast, Ireland.

15

make the ship as comfortable for its passengers as possible. He included several dining rooms, restaurants, and cafés. One of the cafés had real ivy growing up the walls. Another looked just like a sidewalk café in Paris.

The *Titanic* had a grand staircase covered by a glass dome to let in light.

The *Titanic* had a gym with exercise machines and mechanical horses. It also had its own swimming pool—one of the first ever on an ocean liner.

Thomas Andrews tried to make the *Titanic* as safe as possible, too. The ship was built with a double bottom. That meant that anything that hit the bottom would have to rip through two thick layers of steel to cause a leak.

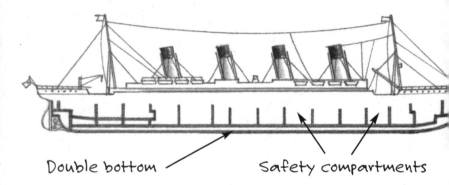

Double bottom   Safety compartments

The lower part of the ship was also divided into 16 parts, or compartments. If an accident caused a compartment to become flooded, it could be sealed off from the rest of the ship. Even if four compartments were flooded, the *Titanic* could stay afloat.

Andrews thought these safety features made the *Titanic* the safest ship on the ocean. Some people even called the *Titanic* "unsinkable."

Getting Ready

Once the *Titanic* was built, it had to be tested. On April 2, 1912, the captain and crew practiced turning the ship left, right, and in a circle. They practiced starting and stopping. They practiced running at different speeds.

After its sea trials, hundreds of workers got the *Titanic* ready for passengers. They finished painting rooms and laying carpets. They loaded tons of food and coal on board.

A ship's tests are called its sea trials.

Finally, on April 10, 1912, the *Titanic* was ready to sail.

Titanic Fact File

Even though its first voyage was scheduled to be only a week long, the *Titanic* needed a *lot* of supplies. Here are some of the things it carried:

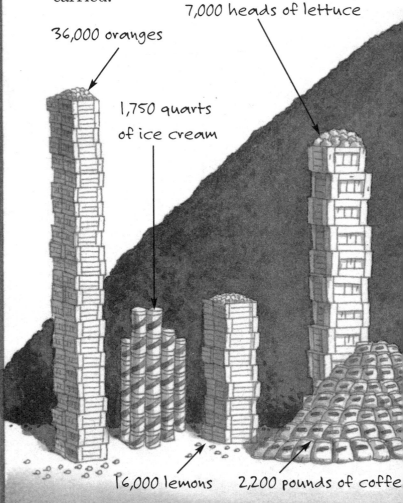

7,000 heads of lettuce

36,000 oranges

1,750 quarts of ice cream

16,000 lemons

2,200 pounds of coffe

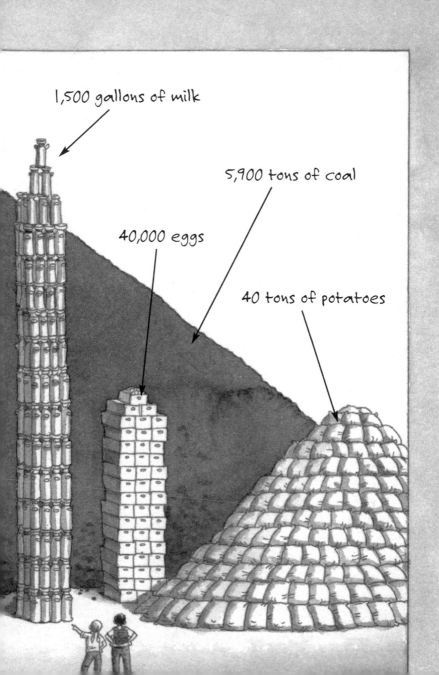

Inside the Titanic

Parisian café

Third-class general room

Third-class cabins

Stern bridge

Rudder

Propellor-shaft tunnel

Freshwater tanks

Here is a peek inside the rear half of the <u>Titanic</u>. Turn the page to see the front half.

À la carte
restaurant

Coal bunker

Second-class
cabins

Aft first-class
staircase

Turbine
engines

Reciprocating
engines

Boilers

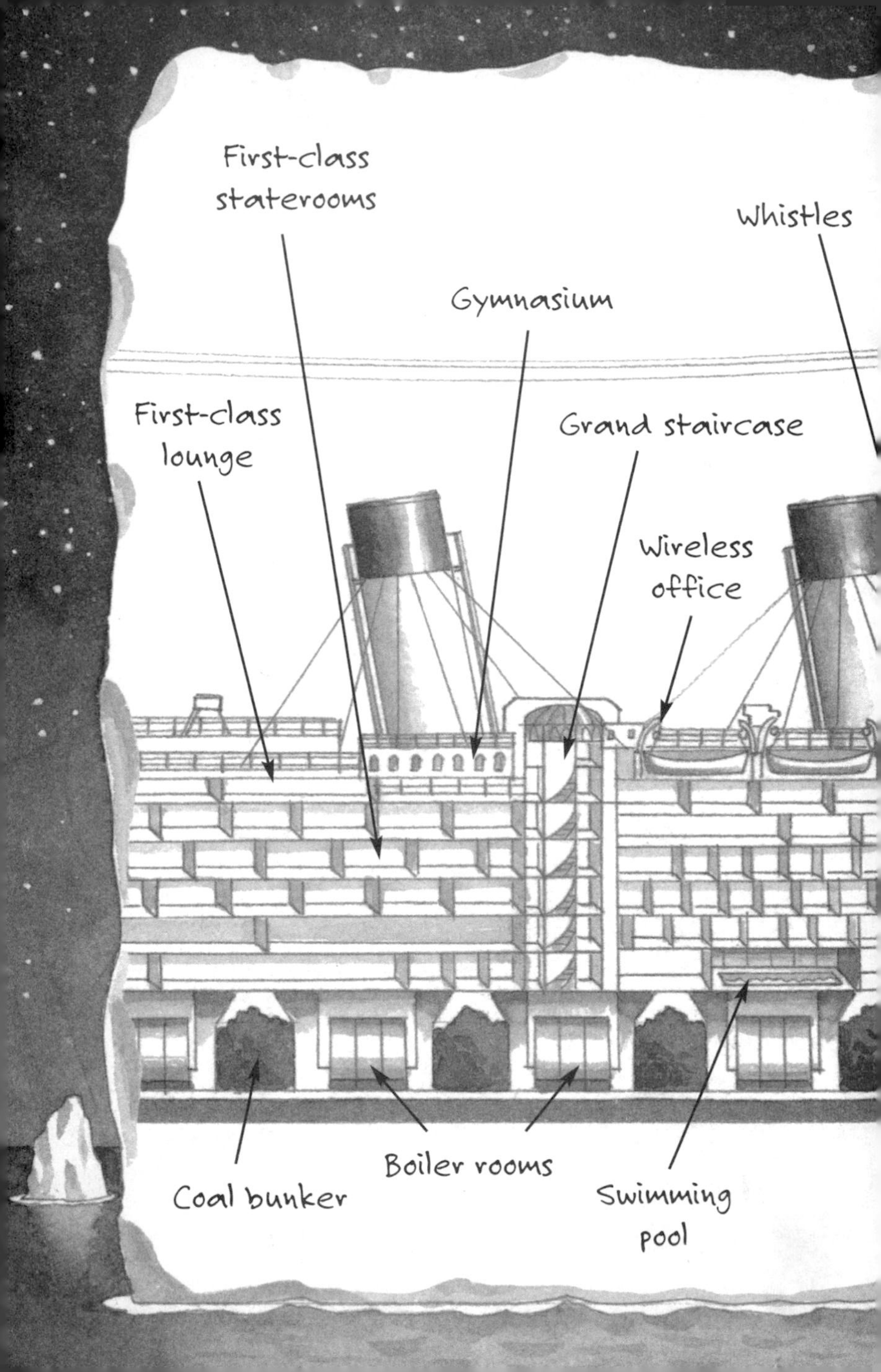

First-class
staterooms

Gymnasium

Whistles

First-class
lounge

Grand staircase

Wireless
office

Coal bunker

Boiler rooms

Swimming
pool

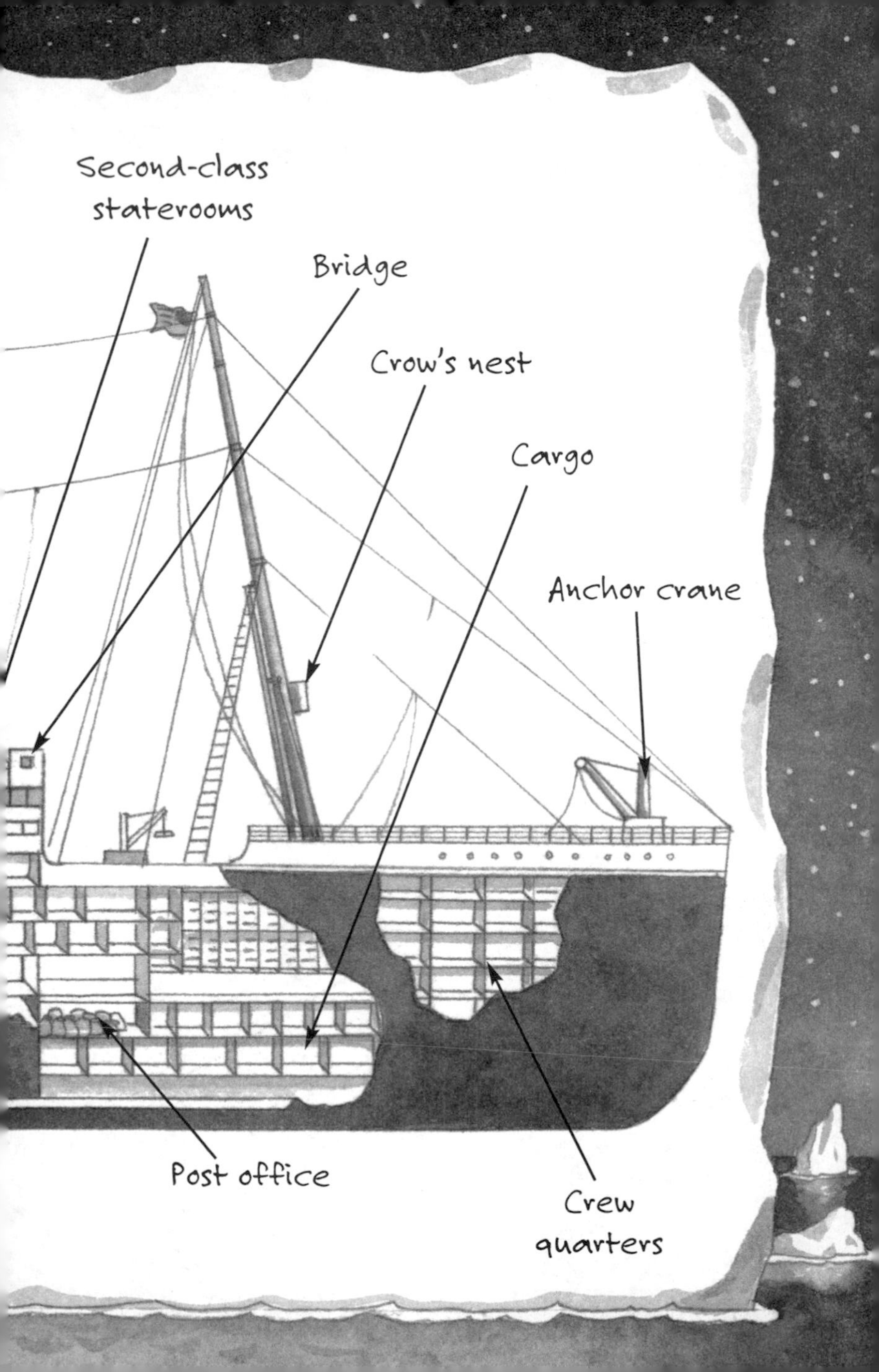

Second-class
staterooms

Bridge

Crow's nest

Cargo

Anchor crane

Post office

Crew
quarters

2

Sailing Day

For its first voyage, the *Titanic* was to sail from Southampton, England, to New York City. It would make stops along the way in France and Ireland. The trip would take about a week.

The captain of the *Titanic* was Edward Smith. Captain Smith had sailed for nearly 40 years with the White Star Line. He was planning to retire after the *Titanic*'s first voyage.

Captain Smith was called "the Millionaire's Captain" because so many rich people enjoyed traveling on his ships.

Captain Smith

Boilers are tanks where water is heated to make steam.

Captain Smith commanded a crew of more than 800 people. There were officers to steer the ship while Captain Smith ate his meals or slept in his cabin. There were engineers in charge of the *Titanic*'s giant engines. There were *stokers* to shovel coal into the *Titanic*'s boilers to keep the engines running. And there were hundreds of workers to take care of the *Titanic*'s passengers.

28

Sixty chefs would cook the passengers' meals. Thirty-six dishwashers would wash up after them. Several hundred *stewards* and *stewardesses* would clean their rooms and wait on them in the dining rooms, restaurants, and cafés.

Titanic steward

The first passenger to come aboard the *Titanic* on April 10 was Thomas Andrews. Andrews arrived at the dock at 6:30 that morning. He wanted to make sure everything on board the ship was perfect.

Andrews worried that some of the deck chairs should be a different color. He thought there were too many screws in some of the hat racks. He wished he had made the library smaller so there could be more rooms for passengers. Still, he must

Most of the *Titanic's* passengers sailed from England, but a few hundred would board the ship in France and Ireland.

There were passengers on the *Titanic* from at least 33 countries.

have been very proud of his ship that day.

Later that morning, other passengers began to arrive. Over 1,300 people had bought tickets to sail on the *Titanic*. Some had business in New York. Others were taking a vacation. Many were moving to America to start a new life.

As the passengers arrived, stewards helped them find their way to their rooms. Rooms on the *Titanic* were divided into three groups—first class, second class, and third class.

First-class rooms were on the upper decks. Nearly all the passengers traveling first-class were very rich. There were bankers, writers, painters, and department store owners. There was a movie actress and a world-famous tennis player.

30

First-class suite

A ticket for a first-class room cost over $400. There were even two sets of first-class rooms that cost $3,300 each—more than a brand-new car cost in those days. These rooms were 50 feet long and had their own private outdoor decks.

Many first-class passengers brought along servants. Most of the servants had rooms near the people they worked for.

In 1912, $400 was worth more than $5,000 in today's money.

31

Some first-class passengers also brought along their pets. There were at least nine dogs and several prize chickens and roosters on the voyage.

Passengers traveling second-class paid much less for their tickets. The average price for a second-class ticket was $65. The rooms in second class were not as fancy as those in first class, but they were still very nice. One young woman wrote that traveling in second class on the *Titanic* was like staying in a first-class hotel.

Second-class room

Third-class room

Most of the *Titanic*'s passengers were traveling in third class. Many of them were *immigrants*. That means they were leaving their home countries to live in America.

Third-class passengers paid about $35 for their tickets. Their rooms were simply furnished, but they were clean and comfortable. They were much nicer than the third-class rooms on other ships of the day.

There were more passengers traveling in third class than in second and first classes combined.

33

The *Titanic* Sails

At a few minutes before noon, crew members took away the walkways leading onto the ship. They dropped the ropes that tied the *Titanic* to the dock. Friends, relatives, and newspaper reporters watched as tugboats pulled the *Titanic* out into the harbor.

Passengers crowded the decks of the ship as it slowly moved toward the sea. They waved goodbye to their friends and families back on the dock.

The *Titanic* blew its whistles. People on the dock cheered. Some blew kisses and waved handkerchiefs.

The *Titanic* was on its way.

Titanic Passengers

Titanic passengers came from all walks of life. Here are just a few of the people who sailed on the ship.

John Jacob Astor

John Jacob Astor was one of the richest men in the world. He was on his way home from his honeymoon in Europe and Egypt with his new wife, Madeleine.

Karl Behr

Helen Newsom

Karl Behr and Helen Newsom had been classmates. Karl was in love with Helen, but her mother did not approve. Helen and her mother boarded the *Titanic* in Southampton. Karl boarded in Cherbourg, surprising Helen's mother! Helen and Karl were married a year after the *Titanic*'s voyage.

Lawrence Beesley was a science teacher in London, England. He was on vacation. He took many notes during the voyage and later wrote a book about it.

Lawrence Beesley

Ruth and Richard Becker

Ruth Becker and Richard Becker were traveling with their mother and sister. They were returning from India, where their father was a missionary.

38

Millvina Dean was the youngest passenger on the *Titanic*—she was only nine weeks old! Her brother, **Bertram**, was almost two. When they grew up, Millvina worked drawing maps and Bertram worked building ships.

Bertram and Millvina Dean

Anna Sofia Turja

Anna Sofia Turja grew up in Finland and spoke no English. She was traveling to Ohio for a job. She shared a room on the *Titanic* with three other immigrants.

39

3

Life on the <u>Titanic</u>

After sailing from Southampton, the *Titanic*'s first stop was Cherbourg, France. The ship arrived at dusk. It picked up more passengers and set sail again at about 8:30 P.M.

Twenty-four passengers and a canary got off the ship at Cherbourg.

    The ship's next stop was Queens-town, Ireland. It arrived there around lunchtime the following day. Over a hundred passengers boarded the ship at

Seven passengers got off the ship at Queenstown.

Queenstown. Most were immigrants traveling in third class.

Then, at around 2:00 P.M. on Thursday, April 11, the *Titanic* steamed out to the open sea and headed for New York.

For the next three days, everything went smoothly. The weather was chilly but beautiful. The ship was making good time. It was even possible that the *Titanic* would arrive in New York ahead of schedule.

This is one of the last known photographs taken of the <u>Titanic</u>.

The passengers spent their days enjoying the ship. Each class had an outside deck, where passengers could go for walks or sit and chat with each other and enjoy the sea air.

Outside decks were called <u>promenades</u> (prah-muh-NAHDZ).

Once the ship was under way, the three classes of passengers were not allowed to mix with each other.

Each of the three classes also had its own dining room. The first-class dining room could seat over 550 people. It was the largest room on any ship at sea!

First-class dining room

First-class passengers could choose from a wide variety of foods at every meal. Among the many dishes on their menus were fresh lobster, roast duckling, fancy puddings, and French ice cream.

The second-class dining room was also very large. Passengers ate together at long tables. The food was similar to the food in first class, but there were fewer choices.

An <u>orchestra</u> is a group of musicians who play together.

During meals, two small orchestras played for the first- and second-class passengers. The musicians also gave concerts in the first- and second-class lounges, where passengers drank, chatted, played cards, and smoked.

The meals in third class were much simpler than those in first and second class. But there was plenty of good, healthy food. Third-class meals included soups, stews, biscuits, potatoes, and desserts.

There was no orchestra for the third-class passengers. Still, there was plenty of entertainment. Several third-class passengers had brought along musical instruments. They often played while other third-class passengers danced.

Since the early 1900s, ships had been using an invention called the wireless. The wireless sent messages using radio waves. These kinds of messages are called *telegrams*.

 This is the only known photo of the Titanic's wireless office.

Many passengers thought it would be a treat for their friends and families to receive a telegram from the biggest ship in the world. They kept the men in the wireless office busy day and night sending messages.

On the first few days of their voyage, the *Titanic*'s passengers had no hint of what was to come. As one first-class passenger later wrote, "I enjoyed myself as if I were in a summer palace on the seashore, surrounded by every comfort."

None of the passengers knew the seas ahead were filled with danger.

Titanic Kids

What did kids on the *Titanic* do for fun? The answer was different for different classes:

Only five children were traveling in first class. They could swim in the swimming pool. They could try out a rowing machine or ride a mechanical horse in the gym.

Twenty-two children traveled in second class. They could play on the second-class deck or read books in the second-class library.

Third class had the greatest number of young passengers—73 children. During the day, they could play on a third-class outdoor deck. One young boy later remembered sneaking down to the lower decks and waving to stokers in the boiler rooms.

4

Iceberg!

As dawn broke on Sunday, April 14, the *Titanic* was heading into dangerous waters. Captain Smith had already received several warnings from other ships that there was ice in the area.

At first, the captain was not overly concerned. There was often ice in the sea lanes between England and America at that time of year.

Sea lanes are the routes ships travel on the ocean.

53

By 2:00 that afternoon, though, Captain Smith had received four more ice warnings. To avoid the ice, he ordered his crew to change the course of the ship. The *Titanic* would now travel farther south than originally planned.

Captain Smith also ordered his lookouts in the crow's nest to keep a careful watch. If they saw any ice, they were to call the bridge at once.

The bridge is the room from which the captain and his officers steer the ship.

Captain Smith thought that if the lookouts spotted ice, there would be time to slow down and steer around it. So he did not reduce the ship's speed.

The crow's nest is a lookout station high above the top deck of a ship.

The weather on Sunday grew colder. By dinnertime, the temperature was just above freezing.

At 7:30, Harold Bride, the *Titanic*'s assistant wireless operator, overheard a message being sent to another ship. The message said there were three large icebergs in the area. He delivered the message to the bridge. Captain Smith was not there. He was having dinner with some of the passengers. He never received the message.

At about 9:00 that night, Captain Smith went to the bridge. The night was clear. The seas were very calm. The *Titanic* was traveling at nearly top speed—about 26 miles per hour.

Captain Smith ordered the officer in charge to slow down only if it became hazy.

"If it becomes at all doubtful, let me know at once," he said. "I shall be just inside." Then he went to his cabin to get ready for bed.

Half an hour later, the wireless room received another ice warning. The message

reported a "great number of large icebergs" in the *Titanic*'s path.

Wireless operator Jack Phillips was very busy. The wireless had broken down the day before. Now he had a big stack of passenger messages to send.

Phillips wrote the ice message down. Then he set it aside. The warning was never delivered to the bridge.

One last ice message came in around 10:55 P.M. It was from a ship not far from the *Titanic*. The message said: "We are stopped and surrounded by ice."

Jack Phillips was still busy sending passenger telegrams. The ice message interrupted his work. He signaled back: "Shut up, shut up, I am busy." No one but Phillips ever got the warning.

Collision

Just before 11:40 P.M., one of the lookouts saw a dark shape sticking out of the sea. It was right in the *Titanic*'s path.

The lookout rang his bell three times, the signal for danger. Then he picked up the phone to the bridge.

"What do you see?" asked the officer in charge.

"Iceberg right ahead!" the lookout shouted back.

The officer on the bridge sent a message to the men in the engine room. He ordered them to slow the ship as quickly as possible. Then he turned the ship's wheel as far as it would go.

There was a pause. Then, slowly, the great ship began to turn.

For a moment, it looked as if the ship might miss the ice completely. Then there was a bump. The bump was followed by a scraping sound.

The *Titanic* had struck the iceberg.

Jack and Annie Present: All About Icebergs

Icebergs are huge, broken-off chunks of glaciers or ice sheets that float on the ocean.

A glacier is a gigantic mass of slowly moving ice that grows over the years.

Icebergs are much bigger than they seem. That's because most of an iceberg floats beneath the surface of the water.

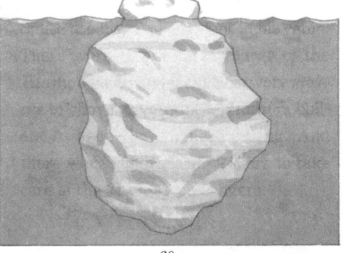

Most icebergs in the Atlantic Ocean come from glaciers in Greenland. Scientists think that's where the iceberg that the *Titanic* struck came from. The "iceberg season" in Greenland lasts from February through October.

This iceberg was photographed on April 15, 1912. Researchers think it might be the iceberg that the <u>Titanic</u> struck.

5

All Hands on Deck

When the *Titanic* struck the iceberg, most passengers didn't even notice the bump. Only a few came out on deck to see if anything was wrong.

In his cabin, Captain Smith *did* feel the bump. He rushed to the bridge. "What have we struck?" he asked.

"An iceberg, sir," his officer replied.

Captain Smith soon got bad news from the ship's carpenter. The ship was

One passenger later said the collision felt as if the ship were rolling over a thousand marbles.

taking on water fast. The mail room and several of the boiler rooms were already flooded.

Captain Smith sent for Thomas Andrews. Andrews was in his room studying drawings of the *Titanic*. He was still trying to think of ways to improve the ship.

Andrews had not felt the jolt or heard the scrape when the ship hit the iceberg. As soon as he heard the news, he ran to the bridge.

Captain Smith and Thomas Andrews went down to check the ship themselves. Andrews could hardly believe it. Six of the safety compartments were filling with water.

The *Titanic* could stay afloat with four flooded compartments—but not with six.

Andrews told Captain Smith the terrible truth: the *Titanic* would sink to the bottom of the ocean within two hours.

Captain Smith ordered his crew to get the *Titanic*'s lifeboats ready. He sent stewards to wake up passengers and bring them out on deck. He said everyone should put on life jackets.

In 1912, life jackets like this one from the Titanic were called life belts.

Then Captain Smith went down to the wireless office. He told Jack Phillips and Harold Bride to start sending out a distress signal.

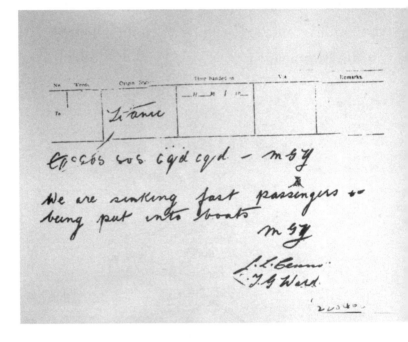

This is a copy of the distress message. It says: We are sinking fast passengers being put into boats.

Captain Smith hoped there would be a ship close enough to come to the rescue before the *Titanic* sank. Earlier in the evening, some of his men had seen the lights of another ship. The ship seemed to be no more than 10 miles away. If the *Titanic* could get word to that ship, perhaps everyone could be saved.

The men in the wireless room began sending the distress signal.

Three ships answered. The closest one was a British passenger ship called the *Carpathia*. It was nearly 60 miles away.

Even traveling at top speed, it would take the *Carpathia* at least three hours to reach the *Titanic*. By then, it would be too late.

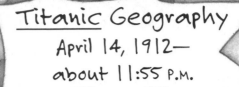

Titanic Geography
April 14, 1912—
about 11:55 P.M.

Titanic

Carpathia

New York

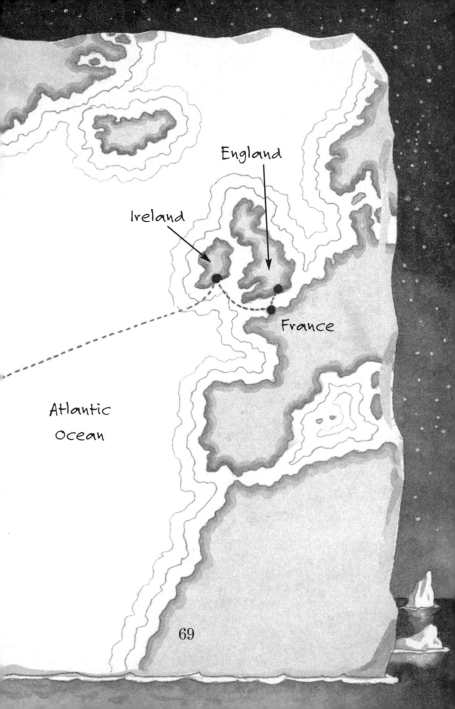

England

Ireland

France

Atlantic
Ocean

6

Into the Lifeboats

As Phillips and Bride continued to send the distress signal, stewards woke the passengers and led them out on deck. At first, hardly anyone believed anything serious had happened. Many passengers came on deck without life jackets. Some refused to come out of their rooms at all. One passenger told a steward, "It will take more than an iceberg to get *me* out of bed."

The passengers stood in the cold wondering what was going on. Some were still in evening clothes. Some wore life jackets over their pajamas.

Several boys played soccer with chunks of ice that had fallen onto one of the decks.

The *Titanic*'s musicians set up their instruments in the lounge near the boat deck. They began playing dance tunes. They hoped their music would help the passengers keep calm.

The stewards didn't want to start a panic. They told the passengers there was nothing to worry about. They said the life jackets were just a precaution. But then crew members started swinging lifeboats over the side of the ship.

It was then that the passengers realized they might be in real danger.

Titanic lifeboats

Women and Children First

Tragically, there was room in the lifeboats for only about half of the people on board the *Titanic*. Safety rules at that time had been made for much smaller ships. The *Titanic* was actually carrying four more boats than the rules called for.

Safety rules said the Titanic could sail with just 16 lifeboats.

The custom of the sea was for women and children to be saved before men. At 12:25 A.M., Captain Smith gave the order: "Women and children first." The crew began calling for women and children to fill the lifeboats.

At first, only a few women wanted to get into the boats with their children. Most didn't want to leave their husbands. The ocean was vast, dark, and cold. The lifeboats seemed tiny. The *Titanic* seemed very large and safe. Though it had already taken on tons of water, it had only begun to slant a tiny bit toward the bow.

The bow is the name for the front end of a ship.

"Lifeboats! What do they need of lifeboats?" said one woman. "This ship could smash a hundred icebergs and not feel it."

When the crew could find no more women and children to fill the first boats, they allowed men to board. Even so, many of the first lifeboats left the ship less than half full.

As the bow of the *Titanic* sank lower and lower, though, people began to realize the lifeboats might be their only hope. More and more of them wanted a place in the boats.

Even though they were afraid, most people behaved bravely. Many men helped their wives and children into boats knowing they might never see them again.

"You go and I'll stay awhile," said one man as he helped his new wife into a boat. When another woman begged her husband to get into a boat with her, he said, "No, I must be a gentleman."

Isidor and
Ida Straus

Some women refused to leave the ship without their husbands. Ida Straus started to board a boat, then turned back. This is what people heard her say to her husband, Isidor:

Titanic Fact File

Is it true that third-class passengers were kept below until the wealthy passengers could get on board the lifeboats?

No. Most third-class rooms were farthest from the deck where the lifeboats were kept. When the *Titanic* began sinking, crew members went to the third-class

"We have been living together for many years. Where you go, I go. As we have lived, so will we die together."

Shortly after 1:00 A.M., the orchestra moved out onto the boat deck. The musicians kept playing as passengers were loaded into the boats. As the ship sank lower and lower, they played hymns.

areas to lead women and children to the boats. Many of the third-class passengers did not speak English. They could not understand what was happening. A large number of women refused to leave their husbands. Sadly, nearly three-quarters of the third-class passengers died in the tragedy.

Every Man for Himself

By about 2:00 A.M., all but two of the lifeboats had left the ship. The last two boats could carry fewer than 50 passengers each. There were over 1,000 people still on board.

The *Titanic* was sinking faster and faster. Captain Smith knew the end was near. He was prepared to go down with his ship.

Captain Smith told the men in the wireless office that the situation was hopeless. They should stop sending the distress message and save themselves if they could. He told the rest of the crew they should do the same. "At this kind of time," he said, "it's every man for himself."

The Mystery Ship

Many passengers and crew members on the *Titanic* said they saw the lights of a ship that seemed much closer than the *Carpathia*.

Why didn't this "mystery ship" come to the *Titanic*'s rescue? No one knows.

The Californian

Many people believe the mystery ship was the *Californian*—the ship that sent the last ice warning to the *Titanic*. The *Californian*'s only wireless operator had gone to bed by the time the *Titanic* struck the iceberg. The *Californian* never received the *Titanic*'s wireless distress signal.

To this day, the identity of the mystery ship is still in question.

7

The <u>Titanic</u> Sinks

As the people in the lifeboats rowed away from the *Titanic*, they saw an amazing sight. The lights of the ship were shining. The orchestra was playing. There were hundreds and hundreds of people on the decks.

But the stern of the ship had risen far out of the water. It looked like the *Titanic* was sliding into the ocean.

The <u>stern</u> is the name for the back end of a ship.

At around 2:15 A.M., two and a half hours after it hit the iceberg, the *Titanic* began to sink very swiftly into the sea. The bow plunged deep under the water. A huge

wave swept over the boat deck. Many of the people still on board were washed into the freezing-cold water. Others tried to climb toward the stern. Some clung to railings. Many jumped into the sea.

As the bow sank deeper and deeper, the *Titanic*'s stern rose farther and farther out of the water. There was a great crash as furniture, pianos, plates, and luggage inside the ship tumbled toward the bow.

People slid off the decks into the water. One of the smokestacks came crashing down. The lights blinked and went out. Then the *Titanic* broke in two!

For a moment, the ship's stern settled back on the water. Then it began to sink rapidly. In another moment, the *Titanic* was gone.

The icy sea was filled with people calling for help. The water temperature was four degrees below freezing. No one could live long in water that cold.

 This painting appeared in a magazine in 1912, shortly after the Titanic sank.

Some of the passengers in the lifeboats wanted to row back to rescue more people. But others were afraid that too many people trying to get into the boats would tip them over—and no one would be saved.

One survivor said that swimming in the icy water felt like being stabbed with a thousand knives.

Finally, two lifeboats did go back to rescue more passengers. They were able to pull nine people from the water. Three of those were so cold, they died within a few hours.

The cries and shouts of the people in the water could be heard for about 20 minutes after the *Titanic* sank. Then all was silent.

People in the lifeboats later said the silence was the saddest thing they had ever heard. It meant their families and friends had died in the freezing water.

Heroes of the Titanic

Many people who sailed on the *Titanic* showed great courage. Here are some *Titanic* heroes.

Molly Brown

Molly Brown helped row the lifeboat she was in. She got the other women in her boat to do the same. When the officer in charge said there was no hope of rescue, she threatened to throw him overboard.

Molly Brown

88

Quartermaster Walter Perkis and Fifth Officer Harold Lowe

Perkis and Lowe commanded the only two lifeboats that went back to try to rescue more people from the water. Together they saved the lives of six more people.

Walter Perkis

Harold Lowe

The *Titanic* Orchestra

Survivors say the orchestra played until after 2:00 A.M., helping to calm many passengers. None of the musicians tried to

Theodore Brailey
pianist

Roger Bricoux
cellist

Georges Krins
violinist

Wallace Hartle
bandmaster

save themselves by getting in a lifeboat. None survived the disaster.

John Clarke
bassist

John Hume
violinist

Percy Taylor
cellist

John Woodward
cellist

8

Rescue

On the night the *Titanic* sank, the *Carpathia* was headed from New York to the Mediterranean Sea. Most of its passengers were on vacation.

The captain of the *Carpathia* was Arthur Rostron. His nickname was "Electric Spark." He was famous for making quick decisions, and for acting on his decisions with energy and enthusiasm.

Captain Rostron

As soon as Captain Rostron heard the *Titanic*'s distress signal, he turned his ship around. He told his crew to gather blankets and make hot coffee and soup. He turned the ship's dining rooms into hospitals. He got lifeboats and rope ladders ready to rescue people from the sea.

Captain Rostron had to steam through dangerous waters to get to the *Titanic*. During the journey, he steered around six icebergs. He kept a careful watch and traveled as fast as he could. Still, the trip took nearly four hours.

By 2:45 A.M., Captain Rostron knew he was drawing near the spot where the

Titanic had gone down. He ordered his men to start firing rockets into the air. He wanted to let the *Titanic* passengers know that help was on the way.

The survivors in the lifeboats saw the rockets from the *Carpathia* at about 3:30 A.M. Many of the survivors were very ill from the cold. A few had broken bones. Some had given up hope of ever being rescued.

As soon as they saw the rockets, people in the lifeboats began to shout and wave. They set newspapers and handkerchiefs on fire so the *Carpathia* could find them in the dark.

Lifeboat rowing toward the <u>Carpathia</u>.

Some <u>Titanic</u> survivors were in the lifeboats for six hours.

The *Carpathia* reached the first lifeboat at about 4:10 A.M. The crew of the *Carpathia* lowered ladders and ropes. They pulled the *Titanic*'s survivors onto their ship. They gave them blankets and hot drinks.

Captain Rostron asked an officer on the first lifeboat if many people had gone down with the *Titanic* when it sank.

"Yes!" said the officer, his voice shaking with emotion. "Hundreds and hundreds! Perhaps a thousand! Perhaps more!"

In all, 706 people were rescued by the *Carpathia* that morning. Over 1,500 had been lost.

The Journey Home

It took over four hours for the *Carpathia* to rescue everyone in the lifeboats. When all were on board, the survivors said a prayer of thanks for having been saved. They held a funeral service for all those who had died. When the service was over, the *Carpathia* headed for New York.

The passengers on the *Carpathia* gave

clothes to the *Titanic* survivors. Many gave up their rooms so the survivors would have a comfortable place to sleep.

Survivors on board the <u>Carpathia</u>.

The voyage to New York took four days. The weather was terrible. There were storms and rough seas. The *Titanic* passengers spent the trip comforting each other and mourning the loss of their loved ones.

People in New York waited for hours for the <u>Carpathia</u> to arrive.

News of the *Titanic* disaster spread quickly all over the world. When the *Carpathia* landed in New York on Thursday evening, 40,000 people were waiting. Among the crowd were the friends and families of the *Titanic*'s passengers and crew. Many did not know if their loved ones had lived or died.

At about 9:00 P.M., the survivors began

to climb down the *Carpathia*'s gangway. Cameras flashed. Reporters shouted questions. Spotlights lit the crowd on the pier to help the survivors find their families and friends.

There were joyful reunions. But there

was also great sadness. Many people were waiting on the pier for friends and family members who had died in the disaster. When the last survivors left the *Carpathia*, these people realized they would never see their loved ones again.

Titanic Timetable

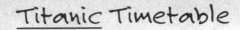

April 10, 1912: Noon—<u>Titanic</u> leaves Southampton, England.

April 10: 6:30 P.M.—<u>Titanic</u> stops in Cherbourg, France.

April 11: 11:30 A.M.—<u>Titanic</u> stops in Queenstown, Ireland.

April 11–April 14—<u>Titanic</u> travels toward New York. Passengers enjoy journey.

April 14: 11:40 P.M.—<u>Titanic</u> strikes iceberg.

April 15: 12:25 A.M.—Passengers begin to be loaded into lifeboats.

April 15: 2:20 A.M.—<u>Titanic</u> sinks.

April 15: 4:10 A.M.—<u>Carpathia</u> reaches survivors.

April 15–April 18—<u>Carpathia</u> sails toward New York.

April 18: 9:00 P.M.—Survivors arrive in New York.

9

Lessons from the Titanic

Once the *Carpathia* landed safely in New York, people wanted to know how the *Titanic* disaster could have happened.

Newspapers interviewed the survivors. The governments of the United States and England held hearings. Why did the "unsinkable" *Titanic* sink on its first voyage? Why weren't more of the

A **hearing** is an official investigation of a situation or event.

passengers and crew saved? Who was to blame?

The hearings found that no one person was to blame for the disaster. The sinking of the *Titanic* was a terrible accident.

But even today, people continue to ask many "what if" questions.

What if all the ice warnings had been delivered to the bridge?

What if Captain Smith had slowed down?

What if there had been enough lifeboats for all the passengers and crew?

We will never know the answers to these questions. But the world learned an important lesson from the *Titanic*. *No* ship is unsinkable. After the *Titanic* disaster, governments passed laws to make traveling on the ocean safer.

Today, passenger ships must travel with enough lifeboats to carry *more* than the number of people on board.

There must be lifeboat drills so passengers and crew can practice what to do in case of an accident.

A <u>drill</u> is a practice session.

Ships crossing the Atlantic during winter and spring months travel even farther south to avoid ice.

All ships traveling on the ocean must keep their radios on at all times to hear distress signals from other ships.

Shipping Rules Today

Lifeboats for everyone

Lifeboat drills

Travel farther south in
    winter and spring

Radios on at all times

International Ice Patrol ship

The International Ice Patrol

Soon after the *Titanic* disaster, the International Ice Patrol was formed. The Ice Patrol looks for icebergs in the Atlantic

Ocean. It warns ships of danger. Every year on April 15, the International Ice Patrol drops wreaths of flowers near the spot where the *Titanic* went down. The flowers are to remember all the lives that were lost that terrible night in 1912.

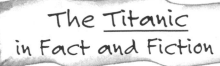

The <u>Titanic</u> in Fact and Fiction

The story of the *Titanic* captured the imagination of the world.

Many books were written by *Titanic* survivors. Hundreds more have been written by researchers and historians interested in the disaster.

The tragedy has also been the subject of several plays and many movies.

The most recent *Titanic* movie, released in 1997, won 11 Academy Awards.

10

Finding the **Titanic**

After the *Titanic* went down, many people dreamed of finding the sunken ship. For more than 70 years, though, no one could locate the *Titanic* on the ocean floor.

Then, in August 1985, an oceanographer named Robert Ballard set out on a new search. Dr. Ballard and his team were testing an underwater device called the *Argo*.

An **oceanographer** is a scientist who studies the ocean.

Dr. Ballard was part of a joint French and American team trying to find the <u>Titanic</u>.

Dr. Robert Ballard

The *Argo* traveled along the ocean floor. Video cameras attached to the *Argo* could send pictures to a ship above.

For weeks, the *Argo*'s video cameras saw nothing but miles and miles of mud.

On September 1, four members of Dr. Ballard's team began the midnight watch. After about an hour, one of the men wondered aloud how they would stay awake. As usual, the video from the *Argo* had been very boring.

The other men didn't answer. Their eyes were glued to the video screen.

"There's something," one said.

Everyone stared at the screen. They saw small shapes scattered across the seabed. The shapes looked as if they could be wreckage from a ship.

Then a large, round object appeared on the screen.

"It's a boiler!" said one of the men.

Dr. Ballard's partner, Jean-Louis Michel, opened a book and found a picture of the *Titanic*'s boilers. He looked from page to screen and back again. He could hardly believe his eyes.

Seventy-three years after the *Titanic* had sunk, the remains of the great ship had been found.

The <u>Titanic</u> was two and a half miles below the surface of the ocean!

The following summer, Dr. Ballard returned to the site. This time, he brought along a mini-submarine called the *Alvin*.

Dr. Ballard and two mini-sub pilots

 It took the <u>Alvin</u> two hours to get from Dr. Ballard's ship down to the ocean floor.

traveled down to the bottom of the ocean. They landed the *Alvin* on one of the *Titanic*'s decks. With the help of a small robot camera, they took close-up videos of the wreck.

Dr. Ballard described the robot video camera as a "swimming eyeball."

117

Dr. Ballard's discovery answered an important question about the *Titanic*. Survivors had reported that the ship broke into two pieces when it sank. But many ex-

perts believed the ship had sunk in one piece. Ballard's expedition proved that the survivors were right—the two halves of the *Titanic* were found almost 2,000 feet apart on the ocean floor.

Dr. Ballard also learned that over the years much of the *Titanic* had been destroyed. Deep-sea creatures had eaten everything made of paper and cloth and almost everything made of wood.

Plate

Cooking pot

Bottle

Among the hundreds of things Dr. Ballard did find were cooking pots, china from the dining rooms, and a doll's head. He also found pieces of deck furniture and a broken chandelier.

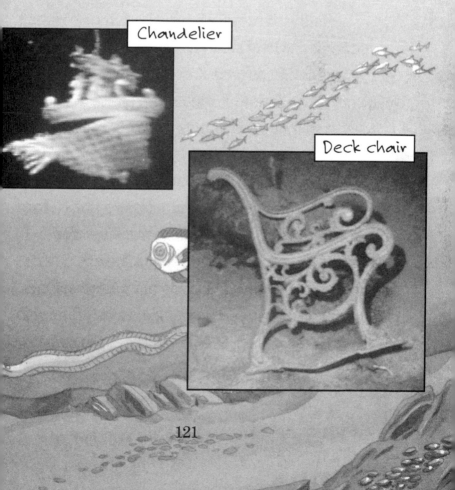

Chandelier

Deck chair

Dr. Ballard recorded many hours of video. He took hundreds of photographs. But he did not bring anything up from the wreckage. He asked future explorers to leave the *Titanic* remains in peace.

Sadly, later expeditions did not treat the site with the same respect. They took away many objects. This led to a great outcry from the public. One survivor called the people who took things from the wreckage "vultures and pirates."

Now many people want the site to be protected as a memorial. They agree with Dr. Ballard that this is the best way to honor the lives that were lost nearly a century ago.

"The bottom of the ocean is a quiet place," Dr. Ballard has written, "a peaceful place, fitting for a memorial to all the things that sank when the *Titanic* went down."

Doing More Research

There's a lot more you can learn about the *Titanic*. The fun of research is seeing how many different sources you can explore.

Books

Most libraries and bookstores have books about the *Titanic*.

Here are some things to remember when you're using books for research:

1. You don't have to read the whole book. Check the table of contents and the index to find the topics you're interested in.

2. Write down the name of the book. When you take notes, make sure you write

down the name of the book in your note-book so you can find it again.

3. Never copy exactly from a book.
When you learn something new from a book, put it in your own words.

4. Make sure the book is <u>nonfiction</u>.
Some books tell make-believe stories of true events that took place in history. These books are called historical fiction. They can help you understand a time and a place, but they don't always have true facts.

Research books have facts and tell true stories. They are called *nonfiction*. A librarian or teacher can help you make sure the books you use for research are nonfiction.

Here are some good nonfiction books about the <u>Titanic</u>:

- *882 ½ Amazing Answers to Your Questions about the <u>Titanic</u>* by Hugh Brewster and Laurie Coulter

- *Finding the <u>Titanic</u>* by Robert D. Ballard

- *<u>Titanic</u>*, Eyewitness Book series, by Simon Adams

- *<u>Titanic</u>: An Illustrated History* by Don Lynch

- *The <u>Titanic</u>: Lost . . . and Found* by Judy Donnelly

Here are some more resources for fun research:

- *Inside the <u>Titanic</u>, a Giant Cutaway Book*, by Ken Marschall

- *<u>Titanic</u>: The Ship of Dreams* by Ken Geist

- *The <u>Titanic</u> Collection: Mementos of the Maiden Voyage* by Hugh Brewster and Eric Sauder (A steamer trunk full of replicas of tickets, menus, maps, and more!)

DVDs

There are some great nonfiction DVDs about the *Titanic*. As with books, make sure the DVDs you watch for research are nonfiction!

Check your library or video store for these and other nonfiction <u>Titanic</u> titles:

- *Secrets of the <u>Titanic</u>*
  from National Geographic

- *<u>Titanic</u>: The Complete Story*
  from The History Channel

- *<u>Titanic</u>'s Final Moments: Missing Pieces*
  from The History Channel

The Internet

Many websites have facts about the *Titanic* and its passengers and crew.

Ask your teacher or your parents to help you find more websites like these:

- britannica.com/titanic

- encyclopedia-titanica.org

- history.com/topics/titanic

- nationalgeographic.com/media/world /9607/titanic.html

Good luck!

Index

Enough cool facts to fill a tree house!

Jack and Annie have been all over the world in their adventures in the magic tree house. And they've learned lots of incredible facts along the way. Now they want to share them with you! Get ready for a collection of the weirdest, grossest, funniest, most all-around amazing facts that Jack and Annie have ever encountered. It's the ultimate fact attack!

*Have you read the adventure that
matches up with this book?*

Don't miss

Magic Tree House® #17

TONIGHT ON THE TITANIC

Jack and Annie are in for an exciting, scary,
and sad adventure when the magic tree house
whisks them back to the decks of the *Titanic*.
Will they be able to save anyone? Will they
be able to save *themselves*?

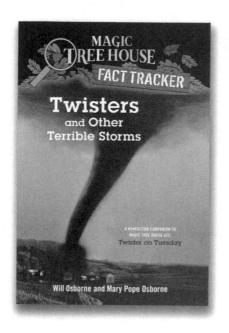

Magic Tree House®

Magic Tree House® Merlin Missions

Magic Tree House® Super Edition

#1: World at War, 1944

Magic Tree House® Fact Trackers

Dinosaurs

Knights and Castles

Mummies and Pyramids

Pirates

Rain Forests

Space

Titanic

Twisters and Other Terrible Storms

Dolphins and Sharks

Ancient Greece and the Olympics

American Revolution

Sabertooths and the Ice Age

Pilgrims

Ancient Rome and Pompeii

Tsunamis and Other Natural Disasters

Polar Bears and the Arctic

Sea Monsters

Penguins and Antarctica

Leonardo da Vinci

Ghosts

Leprechauns and Irish Folklore

Rags and Riches: Kids in the Time of Charles Dickens

Snakes and Other Reptiles

Dog Heroes

Abraham Lincoln

Pandas and Other Endangered Species

Horse Heroes

Heroes for All Times

Soccer

Ninjas and Samurai

China: Land of the Emperor's Great Wall

Sharks and Other Predators

Vikings

Dogsledding and Extreme Sports

Dragons and Mythical Creatures

World War II

More Magic Tree House®

Games and Puzzles from the Tree House

Magic Tricks from the Tree House

My Magic Tree House Journal

Magic Tree House Survival Guide

Animal Games and Puzzles

Magic Tree House Incredible Fact Book

A. R S.1